AN INTRODUCTION TO POETRY

Poems Selected by

Lloyd Cole

GW00802206

1992

Lloyd Cole

MAIDENHEAD

First Published 1992

Lloyd Cole
37 College Avenue
Maidenhead, SL6 6AZ

ISBN 1 874052 16 6 hbk
      1 874052 17 4 pbk

British Library Cataloguing in Publication Data
A catalogue record is available
from the British Library

Printed in Great Britain

Also by Lloyd Cole

Let Me Die
Safe Driving
A New Life of Jesus
In Defence of Private Enterprise
My Baby, My Body, My Choice
The Philosophy of George Bernard Shaw
Successful Selling
Mr Churchill and the Church
Modern Miracles
The Chinese Prince
The Windsor Story
Ye Gods

Compiler of the Solvit Crossword Puzzle Series
and What Do You Know? Crossword Puzzles

PREFACE

Poetry, once discovered, is one of the greatest sources of romance, and of the better understanding of all aspects of life. This is no surprise of course, as good poetry wells up from the experience and faith of the poet. Good poetry is never dull. Good poetry will give you confidence or will make you cry. Poetry will teach you to live by building up inside you a true love of the good in the world.

A great deal of poetry is mumbo-jumbo, utterly ununderstandable by the average man. This is boring rubbish and is the cause of so many disliking poetry. I have not included any of this twaddle.

If you would appreciate the world to the full, read poetry. Try this small personal selection. This selection in part brings tears to my eyes yet in many ways bolsters up my faith in myself and my hopes for the future. Some of this poetry shows me how much better a man I could be, and it also makes me want to be better than I am.

I never met a brute who read poetry.

Lloyd Cole

JOSEPH ADDISON

'Tis not in mortals to command success
But we'll do more, we'll deserve it.

— — —

Content thyself to be obscurely good
When vice prevails, and impious men bear sway,
The post of honour is a private station.

For whereso'er I turn my ravished eyes,
Gay gilded scenes and shining prospects rise,
Poetic fields encompass me around,
And still I seem to tread on classic ground.

In all thy humours, whether grave or mellow,
Thou'rt such a touchy, testy, pleasant fellow;
Has so much wit, and mirth, and spleen about thee,
There is no living with thee, nor without thee.

CHARLES HAMILTON AIDE

I sit beside my lonely fire,
And pray for wisdom yet —
For calmness to remember
Or courage to forget.

ARTHUR CAMPBELL AINGER

God is working his purpose out as year succeeds to year,
God is working his purpose out and the time is drawing near;
Nearer and nearer draws the time,
the time that shall surely be,
When the earth shall be fill'd with the glory of God as
the waters cover the sea.

HENRY ALDRICH

If all be true that I do think,
There are five reasons we should drink;
Good wine — a friend — or being dry —
Or lest we should be by and by —
Or any other reason why.

JOHN ARMSTRONG

Virtuous and wise he was, but not severe;
He still remembered that he once was young.
Of right and wrong he taught
Truths as refin'd as ever Athens heard;
And (strange to tell) he practised what he preached.

MATHEW ARNOLD

We do not what we ought;
What we ought not, we do;
And lean upon the thought
That chance will bring us through.

— — —

I must not say that thou wast true,
Yet let me say that thou wast fair;
And they, that lovely face who view
Why should they ask if truth be there

— — —

Cruel, but composed and bland,
Dumb, inscrutable and grand,
So Tiberius might have sat,
Had Tiberius been a cat.

— — —

Resolve to be thyself: and know, that he
Who finds himself, loses his misery.

— — —

And see all sights from pole to pole,
And glance, and nod, and bustle by;
And never once possess our soul
Before we die.

— — —

Passionate, absorbing, almost blood-thirsty
clinging to life.

SIR ROBERT AYTOUN

I loved thee once, I'll love no more,
Thine be the grief, as is the blame;
Thou are not what thou wast before,
What reason I should be the same?

EDWARD BANGS

Yankee Doodle, keep it up,
Yankee Doodle Dandy;
Mind the music, and the step,
And with the girls be handy.

REV. RICHARD HARRIS BARHAM

A servant's too often a negligent elf;
If its business of consequence, do it Yourself.

SIR JAMES MATHEW BARRIE

Oh the gladness of her gladness when she's glad
And the sadness of her sadness when she's sad
But the gladness of her gladness
And the sadness of her sadness
Are as nothing, Charles,
To the badness of her badness when she's bad.

ELGAR BATEMAN

Wiv a ladder and some glasses
You could see to 'Ackney Marshes,
If it wasn't for the houses in between.

RICHARD BAXTER

In necessary things, unity,
In doubtful things, liberty;
In all things, charity.

— — —

I preached as never sure to preach again,
And as a dying man to dying men!

THOMAS LOVELL BEDDOES

If thou wilt ease thine heart
Of love and all its smart,
The sleep, dear, sleep.

But wilt thou cure thine heart
Of love and all its smart
Then die, dear, die.

− − −

How many times do I love thee, dear?
Tell me how many thoughts there be.

− − −

If there were dreams to sell,
Merry and sad to tell,
And the crier rung the bell
What would you buy?

HILAIRE BELLOC

Of courtesy — it is much less
Than courage of heart or holiness;
Yet in my walks it seems to me
That the grace of God is in courtesy.

— — —

From quiet homes and first beginning,
Out to the undiscovered ends,
There's nothing worth the wear of winning,
But laughter and the love of friends.

— — —

When I am dead, I hope it may be said:
His sins were scarlet, but his books were read.

— — —

If I ever become a rich man,
Or if ever I grow to be old,
I will build a house with deep thatch,
To shelter me from the cold,
And there shall the Sussex songs be sung
And the story of Sussex told,
I will hold my house in the high wood,
Within a walk of the sea,
And the men that were boys when I was a boy
Shall sit and drink with me.

ARTHUR CHRISTOPHER BENSON

Land of Hope and Glory, Mother of the Free,
How shall we extol thee, who are born of thee?
Wider still and wider shall they bounds be set;
God who made thee mighty, make thee mightier yet.

EDMUND CLERIHEW BENTLEY

What I like about Clive
Is that he is no longer alive,
There is a great deal to be said
For being dead.

— — —

Edward the Confessor
Slept under the dresser
When that began to pall
He slept in the hall.

ISAAC BICKERSTAFFE

There was a jolly miller once
Lived on the river Dee;
He worked and sang from morn to night;
No lark more blythe than he.

And this the burden of his song
For ever us'd to be,
I care for nobody, not I
If no one cares for me.

WILLIAM BLAKE

The errors of a wise man make your rule
Rather than the perfections of a fool.

— — —

Every harlot was a virgin once.

— — —

To see a world in a grain of sand,
And a heaven in a wild flower,
Hold infinity in the palm of your hand,
And eternity in an hour.

— — —

A robin redbreast in a cage
Puts all heaven in a rage.

— — —

Love seeketh not itself to please.

— — —

Mutual forgiveness of each vice
Such are the gates of paradise.

— — —

Both read the Bible day and night
But thou read'st black where I read white.

— — —

A truth thats told with bad intent
Beats all the lies you can invent.

— — —

I care not whether a man is good or evil; all that I care
Is whether he is a wise man or a fool. Go! Put off holiness,
And put on intellect.

EDMUND BLUNDEN

All things they have in common being so poor,
And their one fear, death's shadow at the door.
Each sundown makes them mournful, each sunrise
Brings back the brightness in their failing eyes.

FRANCIS WILLIAM BOURDILLON

The night has a thousand eyes,
  And the day but one;
Yet the light of the bright world dies,
  With the dying sun.
The mind has a thousand eyes,
  And the heart but one;
Yet the light of a whole life dies,
  When love is done.

CHARLES BARON BOWEN

The rain it raineth on the just
And also on the unjust fella:
But chiefly on the just, because
The unjust steals the just's umbrella.

RICHARD BRATHWAITE

To Banbury came I, O profane one
Where I saw a Puritane-one
Hanging of his cat on Monday,
For killing of a mouse on Sunday.

ROBERT BRIDGES

I wonder, bathed in joy complete,
How love so young could be so sweet.

J. BROMFIELD

'Tis a very good world we live in,
To spend, and to lend, and to give in;
But to beg, or to borrow, or ask for our own,
'Tis the very worst world that ever was known.

ANNE BRONTË

Because the road is rough and long,
Shall we despise the skylark's song.

RUPERT BROOKE

Unfading moths, immortal flies,
And the worm that never dies.
And in that heaven of all their wish
There shall be no more land, say fish.

ROBERT BROWNING

Ignorance is not innocence but sin.

— — —

'Twas a thief said the last kind word to Christ:
Christ took the kindness and forgave the theft.

— — —

All the breath and the bloom of the year in the gag of one bee.

— — —

I said — Then, dearest, since 'tis so,
Since now at length my fate I know,
Since nothing all my love avails,
Since all, my life seemed meant for, fails,
Since this was written and needs must be —
My whole heart rises up to bless
Your name in pride and thankfulness!
Take back the hope you gave, I claim
Only a memory of the same.

— — —

Measure your mind's height by the shade it casts.

— — —

Vows can't change nature, Priests are only men.

ARTHUR BULLER

There was a young lady named Bright,
Whose speed was far faster than light;
  She set out one day
  In a relative way,
And returned home the previous night.

ROBERT BURNS

Man's inhumanity to man
Makes countless thousands mourn.

— — —

O, My Luv's like a red red rose
That's newly sprung in June:
O my Luv's like the melodie
That's sweetly play'd in tune.

HENRY BURTON

Have you had a kindness shown?
  Pass it on!
'Twas not given for thee alone
  Pass it on!
Let it travel down the years,
Let it wipe another's tears.

LORD BYRON

I am ashes where once I was fire.

— — —

Where virgins are soft as the roses they twine,
And all, save the spirit of man, is divine.

— — —

A little still she strove, and much repented,
And whispering, 'I will ne'er consent', consented.

— — —

Pleasure's a sin and sometimes sin's a pleasure.

— — —

Christians have burnt each other, quite persuaded
That all the Apostles would have done as they did.

— — —

Man's love is of man's life a thing apart
'Tis woman's whole existence.

— — —

Love is heaven and heaven is love.

— — —

Now hatred is by far the longest pleasure
Men love in haste, but they detest at leisure.

— — —

A lovely being, scarcely form'd or moulded,
A rose with all its sweetest leaves yet folded.

LORD BYRON

I hate to run down a tired metaphor.

— — —

Friendship is love without its wings.

— — —

And if I laugh at any mortal thing
'Tis that I may not weep.

— — —

A man must serve his time to every trade
Save censure — critics are all ready made.

— — —

With just enough of learning to misquote.

— — —

... as he knew not what to say, he swore.

HENRY JAMES BYRON

Life's too short for chess.

JAMES BRANCH CABELL

The optimist claims that we live in the best of all
possible worlds; and the pessimist fears this is true.

THOMAS CAMPBELL

To live in hearts we leave behind
Is not to die.

— — —

'Tis distance lends enchantment to the view.

— — —

The proud, the cold untroubled heart of stone
That never mused on sorrow but its own.

GEORGE CANNING

A steady patriot of the world alone
The friend of every country but his own.

— — —

Give 'em the avowed, erect and manly foe;
Firm I can meet, perhaps return the blow;
But of all plagues, good Heaven, they wrath can send,
Save me, oh, save me, from the candid friend.

THOMAS CAREW

Give me more love or more disdain;
The torrid or the frozen zone:
Bring equal ease unto my pain;
The temperate affords me none.

LEWIS CARROLL

How doth the little crocodile
Improve his shining tail.
How cheerfully he seems to grin,
How neatly spreads his claws,
And welcomes little fishes in
With gently smiling jaws!

— — —

A cat may look at a King.

HUGHIE CHARLES

There'll always be an England
While there's a country lane,
Wherever there's a cottage small
Beside a field of grain.

G.K. CHESTERTON

The righteous minds of innkeepers
Induce them now and then
To crack a bottle with a friend
Or treat unmoneyed men,
But who hath seen the grocer
Treat housemaids to his teas
Or crack a bottle of fish-sauce
Or stand a man a cheese?

— — —

And I dream of the days when work was scrappy,
And rare in our pockets the mark of the mint,
And we were angry and poor and happy,
And proud of seeing our name in print.

ALBERT CHEVALIER

We've been together now for forty years
An' it don't seem a day too much;
There ain't a lady livin' in the land
As I'd swop for my dear old Dutch.

CHARLES CHURCHILL

Greatly his foes he dreads, but more his friends;
He hurts me most who lavishly commends.

— — —

Be England what she will
With all her faults, she is my country still.

— — —

By different methods different men excel
But where is he who can do all things well.

— — —

Genius is of no country.

— — —

With the permissive language of a tear.

ARTHUR HUGH CLOUGH

If hopes were dupes, fears may be liars;
It may be, in yon smoke concealed,
Your comrades chase e'en now the fliers,
And, but for you, possess the field.

For while the tired waves, vainly breaking,
Seem here no painful inch to gain,
Far back through creeks and inlets making
Comes silent, flooding in, the main.

And not by eastern windows only,
When daylight comes, comes in the light,
In front the sun climbs slow, how slowly,
But westward, look, the land is bright.

'There is no God' the wicked saith
'And truly it's a blessing,
For what he might have done with us
It's better only guessing.'
But country folk who live beneath
The shadow of the steeple;
The parson and the parson's wife,
And mostly married people.
Youths green and happy in first love,
So thankful for illusion;
And men caught out in what the world
Calls guilt, in first confusion;
And almost everyone when age,
Disease, or sorrows strike him,
Inclines to think there is a God,
Or something very like Him.

— — —

Thou shalt not kill, but need'st not strive
Officiously to keep alive.

— — —

Say not the struggle naught availeth
The labour and the wounds are vain,
The enemy faints not, nor faileth,
And as things have been, things remain.

SAMUEL TAYLOR COLERIDGE

'Tis sweet to him who all the week
Through city-crowds must push his way,
To stroll alone through fields and woods,
And hallow thus the Sabbath day.

— — —

Swans sing before they die — 'twere no bad thing
Did certain persons die before they sing.

— — —

All thoughts, all passions, all delights,
Whatever stirs this mortal frame,
All are but ministers of love,
And feed his sacred flame.

MORTIMER COLLINGS

A man is as old as he's feeling
A woman as old as she looks.

WILLIAM CONGREVE

Music has charms to sooth a savage breast.

— — —

Heaven has no rage, like love to hatred turned,
Nor Hell a fury, like a woman scorned.

— — —

Beauty is the Lover's gift

ABRAHAM COWLEY

Life is an incurable disease.

— — —

Lukewarmness I account a sin
As great in Love as in Religion.

WILLIAM COWPER

He found it inconvenient to be poor.

— — —

... remember, if you mean to please,
To press your point with modesty and ease.

— — —

A noisy man is always in the right.

— — —

Men deal with life as children with their play,
Who first misuse, then cast their toys away.

— — —

He likes the country, but in truth must own,
Most likes it, when he studies it in town.

— — —

God made the country, and man made the town.

— — —

Absence of occupation is not rest,
A mind quite vacant is a mind distressed.

— — —

The lie that flatters I abhor the most.

WILLIAM COWPER

There is a pleasure in poetic pains
Which only poets know.

— — —

Variety's the very spice of life.

— — —

Guilty splendour.

— — —

Riches have wings.

— — —

Our severest winter, commonly called spring.

GEORGE CRABBE

Habit with him was the test of truth
It must be right: I've done it from my youth.

— — —

Lo! the poor toper whose untutor'd sense
Sees bliss in ale, and can with wine dispense;
Whose head proud fancy never taught to steer,
Beyond the muddy ecstasies of beer.

— — —

Secrets with girls, like loaded guns with boys,
Are never valued till they make a noise.

GEORGE CRABBE

Who often reads, will sometimes wish to write.

— — —

The wife was pretty, trifling, childish, weak;
She could not think, but would not cease to speak.

— — —

That all was wrong because not all was right.

MRS EDMUND CRASTER

The Centipede was happy quite,
Until the Toad in fun
Said 'Pray, which leg goes after which?'
And worked her mind to such a pitch,
She lay distracted in the ditch
Considering how to run.

RICHARD CRASHAW

To these, whom death again did wed,
This grave's the second marriage-bed.
For though the hand of fate could force
'Twixt soul and body a divorce,
It could not sever man and wife,
Because they both lived but one life.
Peace, good reader, do not weep;
Peace, the lovers are asleep.
They, sweet turtles, folded lie
In the last knot that love could tie.

JOHN DONNE

Love built on beauty, soon as beauty dies.

— — —

O how feeble is man's power
That if good fortune fall,
Cannot add another hour
Nor a lost hour recall!

JOHN DRYDEN

Ah how sweet it is to love,
Ah how gay is young desire!
And what pleasing pains we prove
When we first approach love's fire!
Pains of love be sweeter far
Than all other pleasures are.

When the denial comes fainter and fainter,
And her eyes give what her tongue does deny,
Ah what a trembling I feel when I venture,
Ah what a trembling does usher my joy!

When, with a sigh, she accords me the blessing,
And her eyes twinkle 'twixt pleasure and pain;
Ah what a joy 'tis beyond all expressing,
Ah what a joy to hear, shall we again!

— — —

But Dying is a pleasure
When Living is a pain.

— — —

All heiresses are beautiful.

— — —

Repentance is the virtue of weak minds.

JOHN DRYDEN

Learn to write well, or not to write at all.

— — —

Pains of love be sweeter far
than all other pleasures are.

— — —

Happy the man, and happy he alone,
He, who can call today his own.
He who, secure within, can say,
Tomorrow do thy worst, for I have lived today.

— — —

Love's the noblest frailty of the mind.

— — —

For present joys are more to flesh and blood
Than a dull prospect of a distant good.

— — —

They say everything in the world is good for something.

— — —

All human beings are subject to decay
And, when fate summons, monarchs must obey.

— — —

Errors like straws, upon the surface flow
He would search for pearls must dive below.

— — —

A thing well set will be wit in all languages.

DAVID EVERETT

You'd scarce expect one of my age
To speak in public on the stage;
And if I chance to fall below
Demosthenes or Cicero,
Don't view me with a critic's eye,
But pass my imperfections by,
Large streams from little fountains flow,
Tall oaks from little acorns grow.

EUGENE FIELD

When I demanded of my friend what viands he preferred,
He quoth, 'A large cold bottle, and a small hot bird'.

FITZGERALD

The moving finger writes; and, having writ,
Moves on 'nor all thy Piety and Wit
Shall lure it back to cancel half a line,
Nor all thy tears wash out a word of it.

ROBERT FROST

My apple trees will never get across
And eat the cones under his pines, I tell him.
He only says, 'Good fences make good neighbours'.

JOHN GALSWORTHY

If on a spring night I went by
And God were standing there,
What is the prayer that I would cry
To Him? This is the prayer:
O God of Courage grave,
O Master of the night of spring!
Make firm in me a heart too brave
To ask Thee anything.

JOHN GAY

Wou'd you gain the gentle creature?
Softly, gently, kindly treat her,
Suff'ring is the lover's part.
Beauty by constraint, possessing,
You enjoy but half the blessing,
Lifeless charms, without the heart.

— — —

A miss for pleasure, and a wife for breed.

SIR WILLIAM SCHWENCK GILBERT

When every one is somebodee,
Then no one's anybody.

— — —

There's a fascination frantic
In a ruin that's romantic;
Do you think you are sufficiently decayed?

— — —

Faint heart never won fair lady!
Nothing venture, nothing win —
Blood is thick, but water's thin —
In for a penny, in for a pound —
It's love that makes the world go round!

— — —

My object all sublime
I shall achieve in time —
To let the punishment fit the crime.

GOLDSMITH

Learn the luxury of doing good.

— — —

Little things are great to little men.

ADAM LINDSAY GORDON

Question not, but live and labour
        Till yon goal be won,
Helping every feeble neighbour,
        Seeking help from none;
Life is mostly froth and bubble,
        Two things stand like stone,
Kindness in another's trouble,
        Courage in your own.

HARRY GRAHAM

Auntie, did you feel no pain
Falling from that apple tree?
Would you do it, please again?
'Cos my friend here didn't see.

— — —

Aunt Jane observed, the second time
        She tumbled off a bus,
The step is short from the Sublime
        To the Ridiculous.

— — —

There's been an accident, they said,
Your servant's been cut in half; he's dead!
Indeed! said Mr Jones, and please
Send me the half that's got my keys.

MATTHEW GREEN

Experience joined with common sense,
To mortals, is a providence.

ROBERT GREENE

Ah! What is love! It is a pretty thing,
As sweet unto a shepherd as a king,
    And sweeter too;
For kings have cares that wait upon a crown,
And cares can make the sweetest love to frown,
    Ah then, ah then,
If country loves such sweet desires do gain,
What lady would not love a shepherd swain.

DOROTHY FRANCIS GURNEY

The kiss of the sun for pardon,
The song of the birds for mirth,
One is nearer God's heart in a garden
Than anywhere else on earth.

MAURICE EVAN HARE

There once was a man who said, 'Damn!
It is borne in upon me I am
An engine that moves
In predestinate grooves,
I'm not even a bus, I'm a tram'.

WILLIAM ERNEST HENLEY

In the fell clutch of circumstance,
I have not winced, nor cried aloud:
Under the bludgeonings of chance
My head is bloody, but unbowed.
It matters not how strait the gate,
How charged with punishments the scroll,
My head is bloody, but unbowed.

SIR ALAN PATRICK HERBERT

Let's find out what everyone is doing,
And then stop everyone from doing it.

GEORGE HERBERT

Dare to be true: Nothing can need a lie;
A fault, which needs it most, grows two thereby.

— — —

Be calm in arguing; for fierceness makes
Error a fault and truth discourtesy.

ROBERT HERRICK

I dare not ask a kiss;
I dare not beg a smile;
Lest having that, or this
I might grow pride the while.

No, No, the utmost share
Of my desire, shall be
Only to kiss that air,
That lately kissed thee.

— — —

Gather ye rosebuds while ye may
Old Time is still a flying
And this same flower that smiles today
Tomorrow will be dying.

Then be not coy, but use your time;
And while ye may, go marry:
For having lost but once your prime
You may for ever tarry.

DR BREWSTER HIGLEY

Oh give me a home where the buffalo roam,
Where the deer and the antelope play,
Where seldom is heard a discouraging word
And the skies are not cloudy all day.

EDWARD WALLIS HOCH

There is so much good in the worst of us,
And so much bad in the best of us,
That it hardly becomes any of us
To talk about the rest of us.

BEN JONSON

Drink to me, only, with thine eyes
And I will pledge with mine.

HENRY KING

How lazily time creeps about.

RUDYARD KIPLING

If you can fill the unforgiving minute
With sixty seconds' worth of distance run,
Yours is the earth and everything that's in it,
And which is more — you'll be a man, my son.

RONALD A. KNOZ

There was a young man of Devizes,
Whose ears were of different sizes;
The one that was small
Was no use at all,
But the other won several prizes.

WALTER SAVAGE LANDOR

Goodness does not more certainly make men happy
Than happiness makes them good.

JOHN LILY

If all the earth were paper white
And all the sea were ink
'Twere not enough for me to write
As my poor heart doth think.

LONGFELLOW

Not in the clamour of the crowded street,
Not in the shouts and plaudits of the throng,
But in ourselves, are triumph and defeat.

— — —

Lives of great men all remind us
We can make our lives sublime,
And, departing, leave behind us
Footprints on the sands of time.

— — —

Stay, stay at home, my heart, and rest;
Home-keeping hearts are happiest.

— — —

The men that women marry
And why they marry them, will always be
A marvel and a mystery to the world.

RICHARD LOVELACE

Stone walls do not a prison make
Nor iron bars a cage.

— — —

I could not love thee (dear) so much
Lov'd I not Honour more.

JAMES RUSSELL LOWELL

No man is born into the world, whose work
Is not born with him; there is always work,
And tools to work with all, for those who will:
And blessed are the horny hands of toil!

MACAULEY

Knowledge advances by steps, and not by leaps.

— — —

Nothing is so useless as a general maxim.

GEORGE MACDONALD

Where did you come from, baby dear?
Out of the everywhere into here.
Where did you get your eyes so blue?
Out of the sky as I came through.

DAVID MALLETT

O grant me, Heaven, a middle state,
Neither too humble nor too great;
More than enough, for nature's ends,
With something left to treat my friends.

CHRISTOPHER MARLOWE

It lies not in our power to love or hate,
For will in us is over-ruled by fate.
When two are stripped, long ere the course begin,
We wish that one should lose, the other win;
And one especially do we affect
Of two gold ingots, like in each respect.
The reason no man knows; let it suffice,
That we beheld is censured by our eyes.
Which both deliberate, the love is slight;
Who ever loved, that loved not at first sight?

— — —

... there is no sin but ignorance.

CHARLES ROBERT MATURIN

'Tis well to be merry and wise,
'Tis well to be honest and true;
'Tis well to be off with the old love,
Before you are on with the new.

LEONARD McNALLY

This lass so neat, with smiles so sweet,
Has won my right goodwill,
I'd crowns resign to call thee mine,
Sweet Lass of Richmond Hill.

HUGHES MEARNS

As I was going up the stair
I met a man who wasn't there.
He wasn't there again today
I wish, I wish he'd stay away.

GEORGE MEREDITH

Under yonder beech-tree single on the greensward,
Couched with her arms behind her golden head,
Knees and tresses folded to slip and ripple idly,
Lies my young love sleeping in the shade.

— — —

She whom I love is hard to catch and conquer,
Hard, but O the glory of the winning were she won.

DIXON LANIER MERRITT

A wonderful bird is the pelican,
His bill will hold more than his belican.
He can take in his beak
Food enough for a week,
But I'm damned if I see how the helican.

ALICE MEYNELL

I come from nothing; but from where
Come the undying thoughts I bear.

JOHN MILTON

The finest and wisest of them all professed
To know this only, that he nothing knew.

PERCY MONTROSE

But I kissed her little sister,
And forgot my Clementine.

THOMAS MOORE

Then awake' the heavens look bright, my dear;
'Tis never too late for delight, my dear;
And best of all ways
To lengthen our days
Is to steal a few hours from the night, my dear!

JAMES BALL NAYLOR

King David and King Solomon
Led merry, merry lives,
With many, many lady friends
And many, many wives;
But when old age crept over them,
With many, many qualms,
King Solomon wrote the Proverbs
And King David wrote the Psalms.

JOHN NEWTON

How sweet the name of Jesus sounds
In a believers' ear!
It soothes his sorrows, heals his wounds,
And drives away his fear.

JOHN OWEN

God and the Doctor we alike adore
But only when in danger, not before;
The danger o'er, both are alike requited,
God is forgotten, and the Doctor slighted.

COVENTRY PATMORE

Ah, wasteful woman, she who may
On her sweet self set her own price,
Knowing man cannot choose but pay
How has she cheapen'd paradise;
How given for nought her priceless gift,
How spoil'd the bread, and spill'd the wine
Which, spent with due, respective thrift,
Had made brutes men, and men divine.

JOHN HOWARD PAYNE

Mid pleasures and palaces though we may roam,
Be it so humble, there's no place like home.

JAMES PAYN

I had never had a piece of toast
Particularly long and wide,
But fell upon the sanded floor,
And always on the buttered side.

WINTHROP MACKWORTH PRAED

His talk was like a stream, which runs
With rapid change from rocks to roses:
It slipped from politics to puns,
It passed from Mahomet to Moses;
Beginning with the laws that keep
The planets in their radiany courses,
And ending with some precept deep
For dressing eels, or shoeing horses.

ALEXANDER POPE

Men, some to business, some to pleasure take;
But every woman is at heart a rake.

— — —

The ruling passion, be what it will,
The ruling passion conquers reason still.

— — —

The hungry judges soon the sentence sign,
And wretches hang that jurymen may dine.

— — —

Beauties in vain their pretty eyes may roll;
Charms strike the sight, but merit wins the soul.

MATHEW PRIOR

I court others in verse: but I love thee in prose:
And they have my whimsies, but thou hast my heart.

— — —

They never taste who always drink;
They always talk, who never think.

FRANCIS QUARLES

No man is born unto himself alone;
Who lives unto himself, he lives to none.

— — —

Physicians of all men are most happy;
What good success 'soever they have,
The world proclaimeth,
And what faults they commit, the earth covereth.

— — —

He that hath no cross deserves no crown.

ROBERT CAMERON ROGERS

The hours I spent with thee, dear heart,
Are as a string of pearls to me;
I count them over, every one apart,
My rosary.

CHRISTINA GEORGINA ROSSETTI

My heart is like a singing bird
Whose nest is in a watered shoot;
My heart is like an apple-tree
Whose bows are bent with thickset fruit;
My heart is like a rainbow shell
That paddles in a halcyon sea;
My heart is gladder than all these
Because my love is come to me.

— — —

Better by far you should forget and smile
Than that you should remember and be sad.

FREDERICH VON SCHELLER

Thoughts are free from toll.

SIR WALTER SCOTT

O what a tangled web we weave,
When first we practise to deceive.

SIR CHARLES SEDLEY

Phyllis is my only joy,
Faithless as the winds or seas;
Sometimes coming, sometimes coy,
Yet she never fails to please.
She deceiving,
I believing;
What need lovers wish for more.
Why then should I seek further store,
And still make love anew;
When change itself can give no more,
'Tis easy to be true.

WILLIAM SHAKESPEARE

Let me not to the marriage of true minds
Admit impediments, love is not love
Which alters when it alteration finds,
Or bends with the remover to remove,
O no, it is an ever fixed mark
That looks on tempests and is never shaken;
It is the star to every wandering bark,
Whose worth's unknown, although his height be taken.

HENRY WHEELER SHAW

Thrice is he armed that hath his quarrel just,
But four times he who gets his blow in fust.

— — —

The trouble with people is not that they don't know
But that they know so much that ain't so.

RICHARD SHEALE

For Witherington needs must I wail,
As one in doleful dumps
For when his legs were smitted off,
He fought upon his stumps.

The fountains mingle with the river,
And the rivers with the ocean;
The winds of heaven mix for ever
With a sweet emotion;
Nothing in the world is single;
All things, by a law divine,
In one another's being mingle.
Why not I with thine? —
See the mountains kiss high heaven
And the waves clasp one another;
No sister-flower would be forgiven
If it disdained its brother;
And the sunlight clasps the earth
And the moonbeams kiss the sea:
What are all these kissings worth
If thou kiss not me?

I love all that thou lovest,
Spirit of delight:
The fresh earth in new leaves dressed,
And the starry night;
Autumn evening, and the morn
When the golden mists are born.
I love tranquil solitude,
And such society
As is quiet, wise, and good;
Between thee and me
What difference? but thou dost possess
The things I seek, not love them less.

I love love.

SHELLEY

I arise from dreams of thee
In the first sweet sleep of night,
When the winds are breathing low,
And the stars are shining bright:
I arise from dreams of thee,
And a spirit in my feet
Hath led me — who knows how?
To thy chamber window, Sweet!

Oh lift me from the grass!
I die! I faint! I fail!
Let thy love in kisses rain
On my lips and eyelids pale,
My cheek is cold and white, Alas!
My heart beats loud and fast; —
Oh! Press it to thine own again,
Where it will break at last

— — —

The pleasure of believing what we see.

— — —

I fear thy kisses, gentle maiden,
Thou needest not fear mine;
My spirit is too deeply laden
Ever to burden thine.
I fear thy mien, thy tones, thy motion
Thou needest not fear mine;
Innocent is the hearts devotion
With which I worship thee.

— — —

For she was beautiful — her beauty made
The bright world dim, and everything beside
Seemed like the fleeting image of a shade.

SIR PHILIP SIDNEY

My true love hath my heart and I have his
By just exchange one for the other given;
I hold his dear, and mine he cannot miss.
There never was a better bargain driven.

EDMUND SPENSER

One day I wrote her name upon the strand
But came the waves and washed it away:
Again I wrote it with a second hand,
But came the tide, and made my pains his prey.
Vain man, said she, that doest in vain assay,
A mortal thing so to immortalize,
For I myself shall like to this decay,
And eke my name be wiped out likewise.
Not so, quoth I, let baser things devise
To die in dust, but you shall live by fame:
My verse your virtues rare shall eternize,
And in the heavens write your glorious name,
Where when as death shall all the world subdue,
Our love shall live, and later life renew.

FRANK LEBBY STANTON

Sweetest li'l feller, everybody knows;
Dunno what to call him, but he's mighty lak' a rose;
Lookin' at his mammy wid eyes so shiny blue
Mek you think that Heav'n is comin' clost ter you.

ROBERT LOUIS STEVENSON

The child that is not clean and neat,
With lots of toys, and things to eat,
He is a naughty child, I'm sure —
Or else his dear papa is poor.

NAHUM TATE

To the hills and the vales,
To the rocks and the mountains,
To the musical groves
And the cool shady fountains.
Let the triumphs of love,
And the beauty be shown.

JANE TAYLOR

Who ran to help me when I fell,
And would some pretty story tell,
Or kiss the place to make it well?
My Mother.

LORD TENNYSON

Their's not to make reply
Their's not to reason why
Their's but to do and die
Rode the six hundred.

— — —

Ah! when shall all men's good
Be each man's rule and universal Peace
Lie like a shaft of light across the land.

— — —

Tis better to have loved and lost
Than never to have loved at all.

— — —

Knowledge comes but wisdom lingers.

Her arms across her breast she laid;
She was more fair than words can say:
Bare-footed came the beggar maid
Before the King Cophetua.
In robe and crown the king stept down,
To meet and greet her on the way;
It is no wonder, said the lords,
'She is more beautiful than day.'

As shines the moon in clouded skies,
She in her proud attire was seen:
One praised her ankles, one her eyes,
One her dark hair and lovesome mein.
So sweet a face, such angel grace,
In all that land had never been:
Cophetua swore a royal oath:
'This beggar maid shall be my queen!'

— — —

He that only rules by terror
Doth grevious wrong.

— — —

He is all fault who hath no fault at all
For who loves me must have a touch of earth.

— — —

Go not, happy day,
From the shining fields,
Go not, happy day,
Till the maiden yields.
Rosy is the West,
Rosy is the South,
Rosy are her cheeks,
And a rose, her mouth.

LORD TENNYSON

Oh well for him whose will is strong
He suffers, but he will not suffer long;
He suffers, but he cannot suffer long.

— — —

My strength is as the strength of ten
Because my heart is pure.

— — —

It is better to fight for the good,
Than to rail at the ill.

— — —

There is no joy but calm.

— — —

The greater man, the greater courtesy.

— — —

Sweet is death who puts an end to pain.

THACKERY

Werther had a love for Charlotte
Such as words could never utter;
Would you know how first he met her?
She was cutting bread and butter.

Charlotte was a married lady,
And a moral man was Werther,
And for all the worth of Indies,
Would do nothing for to hurt her.

So he sighed and pined and ogled,
And his passion boiled and bubbled,
Till he blew his silly brains out
And no more was by it troubled.

Charlotte, having seen his body
Borne before her on a shutter,
Like a well-conducted person,
Went on cutting bread and butter.

JOHN WESLEY

Do all the good you can,
By all the means you can,
In all the ways you can,
In all the places you can,
At all the times you can,
To all the people you can
As long as ever you can.

ELLA WHEELER WILCOX

Laugh and the world laughs with you;
   Weep, and you weep alone;
For the sad old earth must borrow its mirth,
   But has trouble enough of its own.

So many Gods, so many creeds,
   So many paths that wind and wind,
While just the art of being kind
   Is all the sad world needs.

OSCAR WILDE

Yet each man kills the thing he loves
By each let this be heard,
Some do it with a bitter look,
Some with a flattering word.

— — —

He who lives more lives than one
More deaths than one must die.

— — —

There is no sin except stupidity.

JOHN WILMOT

Here lies a great and mighty king
Whose promise none relies on;
He never said a foolish thing,
Nor ever did a wise one.

GEORGE WITHER

If she think not well of me,
What care I how fair she be?

ELIZABETH WORDSWORTH

If all the good people were clever,
    And all clever people were good,
The world would be nicer than ever
    We thought that it possibly could.

But somehow, 'tis seldom or never
    The two hit it off as they should;
The good are so harsh to the clever,
    The clever so rude to the good!

WILLIAM WORDSWORTH

I wandered lonely as a cloud
That floats on high o'er vales and hills,
When all at once I saw a crowd,
A host, of golden daffodils.

WILLIAM WORDSWORTH

She was a phantom of delight
A creature not too bright or good
For human nature's daily food;
For transient sorrows, simple wiles,
Praise, blame, love, kisses, tears and smiles.
A perfect woman, nobly planned,
To warn, to comfort, and command;
And yet a spirit still, and bright
With something of angelic light.

— — —

And hark, how blithe the throstle sings!
He, too, is no mean preacher:
Come forth into the light of things,
Let nature be your teacher.
Enough of science and of art;
Close up these barren leaves;
Come forth, and bring with you a heart
That watches and receives.

— — —

Poetry is the breath and fine spirit of all knowledge.
Poetry is the spontaneous overflow of powerful feelings.

SIR HENRY WOTTON

How happy is he born and taught
That serveth not another's will;
Whose armour is his honest thought,
And simple truth his utmost skill!

WILLIAM BUTLER YEATS

But I, being poor, have only my dreams;
I have spread my dreams under your feet;
Tread softly because you tread on my dreams.

— — —

Was there ever dog that praised his fleas?

EDWARD YOUNG

A fool at forty is a fool indeed.

— — —

Who does nothing with a better grace.

— — —

For ever most divinely in the wrong.

— — —

Procrastination is the thief of time.

— — —

All men think all men mortal, but themselves.

IZRAEL ZANGWILL

Scratch the Christian and you find the pagan-spoiled.